The Journey of an Acorn

by

Corey Wolff

For my little acorns:

Always remember that deep

within you lies the seed of

greatness. Nurture it with love.

"The creation of a thousand forests

is in one acorn."

Ralph Waldo Emerson

Deep in the forest there stood an oak tree. And on one of its branches, there hung a little acorn. One day the little acorn decided it was time to separate from the oak tree. "I want to be on my own, so I can put down my roots, and drink from the cool water in the soil, and grow under the open sky, and feel the sun's love on my face," said the acorn.

But the tree was not ready. "You'll never survive on your own. You must stay beside me, so I can protect you," said the tree. Despite the tree's wishes, the little acorn broke free, falling to the earth. But when it hit the bottom, it was surrounded by darkness. And the acorn was cold, and wet. It heard strange noises all around. And it realized that it couldn't move. For the first time, the acorn was afraid.

Eventually, a squirrel came by and began frantically digging a hole. Suddenly it heard a voice say, "Please help me." It was the little acorn laying there, helpless.

"You look sad. Do you need some help?" said the squirrel.

"Please pick me up and take me to a place where I can put down my roots, and drink from the cool water in the soil, and grow under the open sky, and feel the sun's love on my face. Then I can become a big oak tree."

"I'd be happy to take you away from here," said the squirrel.

Just at that moment, the oak tree took its branch and shoved the squirrel onto the ground. "I know what's best for my little acorn. Now shoo." After that, all of the forest animals avoided the little acorn, for they knew the oak tree would send them away.

So the little acorn waited for a long time in the cold, wet, and dark forest, unable to move, hoping for the wind to come and blow it to a distant place.

But the wind was never strong enough. Finally, the little acorn, who realized no one could save it, cracked, putting down its roots beside the big oak tree.

"That's good," said the tree. "Now I can protect you. Do you know how lucky you are? If I didn't love you, you'd have no one to take care of you."

But the tree didn't take care of the acorn at all. Instead it took up most of the sunlight. And it drank up most of the water. And as the days went by, its roots entangled the little acorn and squeezed, not wanting to let go. And the little acorn barely grew. It spent its days watching the birds and squirrels pick up other acorns, take them to different places in the forest, and bury them. And it looked sadly at them from a distance as they began to grow taller and stronger.

One day, a girl was twirling past the little acorn as she made her way through the forest. As she came closer, the little acorn cried, "Please help me; I'm being smothered by this oak tree."

The girl thought she heard a voice, and looked around, but there was no one. Then she looked down and saw the little acorn. "Aww, aren't you a beautiful little tree? But you'll never make it in this shade. I know a nice space you will just love. I will help you!" said the girl. "I'll move you away from here, so you can feel the sun against your tiny leaves, and get all of the water you need." As the girl began digging up the little acorn, the oak swung one of its jagged branches against her cheek, scratching her face.

"Ow," the girl yelled out, as she covered her cheek with her hand.

"What right do you have to take my little acorn from me? Stay away!" said the tree. But the little girl, thinking it was just the blowing of the wind, continued digging.

The oak tree, who was mad at the girl, was also angry at the little acorn for wanting to leave. So it said, "You'll never survive without me," yelling scornfully.

The girl had to rip some of the roots away to separate it. This was traumatizing to the oak tree, for it was scared and didn't know what to do with itself. This was also true for the little acorn, who had never really been on its own before. Once the little acorn was no longer connected to the oak tree, it became sad, for it knew part of itself had been lost. But it also knew that leaving was the only way for it to be free and become a great oak.

The girl took the little acorn out of the forest and planted it in a nearby field, hoping to help it become strong. But its tiny leaves had begun to wilt. It found itself once again in a strange place. And at night, there were creatures which it did not know. It began to think the oak was right; maybe it wouldn't survive on its own.

But it slowly began to heal. As the seasons passed, and as the years went by, it became bigger and stronger. Its roots grew, and grew, and grew. Sometimes the girl would come by and talk to the little acorn. Sometimes she would lean on it when she was sad. Sometimes when she wanted to play, she would dance around it.

And for the first time, the little acorn felt loved. But inevitably, the day came when the girl could no longer stay. "I have always wanted to become a famous dancer and see the world," she said. "It's time for me to leave, so I can follow my dream. Thank you for being there for me to lean on when I needed you, little acorn. I will miss you," she said, as she gave it a great big hug.

The little acorn had always looked forward to the girl's visits, and now she was gone. It thought, "Who will love me? She's not supposed to leave. She needs to give up her dream and come back to be with me." And the acorn was sad.

As time passed, it became thicker and had hardened. And as the days grew colder, it held onto its colorful leaves as tightly as it could, for it was afraid of losing more of itself to the world.

One day there was a great storm. And the leaves on its branches became covered with snow. And its neck bowed under the weight on its crown. Eventually its branches snapped off, leaving only jagged edges. The little acorn was broken. Once again, it had lost part of itself. And this time, it didn't think it could be fixed.

As it looked down, feeling hopeless, it saw a bird's nest that had fallen off of one of its branches. A baby bird who had been pinned down, was struggling to breathe.

"Please he...help me," tweeted the bird frantically. But the acorn felt so sorry for itself that it pretended it couldn't hear the bird's pleas. Finally there was only silence. Eventually the acorn started to wonder what had happened to the baby bird. And it began to worry that it had become too hurt to cry out. So the acorn called to it in the darkness. But there was no answer. It then used what branches it had left to lift up the broken parts of itself, searching for the fragile life underneath. But there was only emptiness.

For many more years, the acorn was alone. During this time, it thought about the little bird whom it could have helped, and it felt a deep sense of regret. It also thought about the girl and how she saved it because of the goodness in her heart. And it realized it was selfish to want to keep her from seeing the world. In fact, it knew it was no better than the oak tree from which it had grown.

The acorn would also spend a lot of time thinking about its early life when it was attached to the oak tree. Back then, it thought the tree had stood tall and straight with lush branches. But now, for a reason it did not understand, it was aware that the tree had not been straight at all. Rather, it was twisted and bent, and it was mostly hollow, and many of its branches had died. One night, when the tree came to the acorn in a dream, the acorn asked, "Oak tree, please tell me what happened to you so long ago. How did you become so damaged?"

The oak tree said, "Long ago, when I was a sapling, I remember the forest as a lonely place. All the trees that surrounded me were concerned only with themselves, taking up the light from the sun and using the water in the soil which I needed to thrive. And I had always stood naked, exposed to the dangers of the world. One night a bolt of lightning, which seemed to come from nowhere, struck me. After that I never could grow inside. Over time my trunk became crooked; for I was sick, and that was all I knew. When you appeared on my branch, I was happy you could finally take care of me and fulfill all of my needs.

For the first time the acorn realized why the tree had been broken from very early in its life and never had the chance to grow properly. "I'm so sorry that happened to you," said the acorn. It now understood that the poor tree had not had much else to hold on to; it decided to stay and comfort it. And suddenly a bud of a leaf began to sprout from one of the oak tree's dead branches.

Then the acorn awoke. It took some time for it to realize where it was. It now felt its roots which were spread out deep in the earth as it watched the shrubs and grass. It felt the wind flowing through its branches and saw the sun slowly moving across the sky. And it heard the rhythmic drops of rain beating against its leaves.

It thought about the oak tree's roots that had once entangled it, depriving it of the nutrients it needed. And it let go. It thought about the little girl who had left it behind. And it let go. It thought about its own branches which had snapped off and now laid before it. And it let go. It thought about the injured baby bird that it had failed to save. And it let go. It thought about the other trees which grew while it had remained a little acorn. And it let go. Then it straightened its trunk as much as it could, and it was at peace. One day its branches started growing its own acorns. And much like when it was just a little fella, they wanted to experience the world. And the acorn said, "Go find your way little ones."

So they dropped to the ground. And they realized they couldn't move. And they felt scared. And they believed they had made a terrible mistake. "Help us get back up on your branches," they said.

"You can no longer be on my branches," said the little acorn.

"Why not?" they asked.

"Have faith. Everything you need to become great oak trees is already within you."

"But how can we do that?" asked one of the acorns."

"When you feel stuck, do not wait for the wind to take you away, for you are too heavy to be blown. When you feel hopeless, do not put down roots where the sun can never shine on you, for you will deprive the world of your beauty. When you find yourself close to those who care only for themselves, do not be drawn in, for they will only take from you. Do not be scared to ask for help from the animals who dwell in the forest, for they are the only ones who can take you under the open sky. Plant yourselves in the right soil, for once you grow your roots, you become part of the earth that surrounds you. Be generous and loving, providing food and shelter to all creatures, and they will in turn provide for you. Be grateful and accepting of what has been offered to you. And most important, it is only when you become detached from all things that you will truly be connected to the world. These are the only gifts I can give to you, for I am old and I cannot follow you on your journey. And you must make the choice to open yourselves up to the world and take in all it has to offer."

The little acorn watched as its offspring slowly entered the great unknown. Gone was the one who had once entangled it. Gone was each of its acorns. Gone was the little girl with whom it talked. Now it felt the sun on the crown of its branches. And it drank water plentifully from its roots. It stood in a clearing, tall and proud, for it was an oak tree.

Made in the USA
Middletown, DE
26 May 2019